SELENIUM BY EXAMPLE –
VOLUME II: SELENIUM RC

ISBN: 978-1-326-01036-2

First Edition. First published in 2014.

SELENIUM BY EXAMPLE

Volume II: Selenium RC

Table of Contents

Contents at a Glance

Table of Contents

Detailed Contents

Chapter 1: Overview of this book

This chapter lays-out the structure of the rest of the book, as well as giving you details of the notation that is used within the book.

This chapter sets-out to give you an overview of the rest of this book, **Selenium By Example – Volume II: Selenium RC**, for the purpose of aiding you, the reader, to navigate easier through the rest of the book, to also show the step-by-step approach to learning Selenium RC that has been taken in the book, and finally to highlight certain notation that is used throughout this book.

This chapter will cover the following items:

- ✓ The aim of this book.
- ✓ The structure of the rest of the book.
- ✓ Notation that is used throughout the book.
- ✓ The approach to learning taken in this book.

1.1 Aim of this book

The aim of this book is to give you, the reader and introduction and foundation in the learning and understanding of Selenium RC Automated Web Testing software.

This book, like any other book, can only hope to give you a good understanding of the topic, and show you how to gain more experience and gain a better understanding of the subject matter.

No book, can give you the knowledge and experience you would gain from using Selenium RC for 1 year, 5 years, or 10 years on a day-to-day basis. But this book aims to give you the foundation that you can build upon, and to also give you the information which over time and through practical hands-on experience will be able to use to complete the tasks you need with Selenium RC.

1.2 Structure of the rest of the book

The rest of this book is broken down into the following chapters. The order of the chapters, has been designed to aid with your learning, and support the approach to learning (via step-by-step tutorials) that this book uses.

The structure of the rest of the book is as follows:

- Chapter 2, sets out what Selenium RC is and what it is capable of doing. This includes giving a background on the Selenium project.
- Chapter 3, takes you through the downloading, installing, and then running of Selenium RC for the first time.
- Chapter 4, introduces the structure of Selenium RC, and how you can use it.
- Chapter 5, takes you step-by-step through the creation of a Selenium RC Test Script.
- Chapter 6, takes you through the execution of the Test Script created in Chapter 5.
- Chapter 7, goes through more advanced Selenium RC Test Script.
- Chapter 8, gives you the Selenium RC functions to use for Elements (both HTML and Web Page).
- Chapter 9, discusses how to identify Web Page Elements.
- Chapter 10, recommends an approach and an structure for Automated Test Scripts.
- Chapter 11, discusses the types of Automation Frameworks available.
- Chapter 12, discusses the benefits and draw-backs of automated testing.
- Chapter 13, talks you through an approach to take for introducing automated testing.

1.3 Notation used in this book

Through-out the rest of this book certain notation is used to aid with the learning of Selenium RC. This notation is used for highlighting important information you need to know about the item; to warn you of potential problems (you should be aware of); and for providing extra information on the given item (which can be used to find further information).

The following Icons are used for each of these (Important Information, Warnings, and More Information):

 This is the icon used to highlight Important Information you need to know.

 This icon is used to give you Warning information.

 This icon is used to highlight More Information on the topic in hand, or to point you in the right direction to find-out more information on the topic.

1.4 Approach to learning

The aim of this book is to be a step-by-step guide for you to learn, understand, and use Selenium RC. The approach taken is two prong. Firstly, to break-down the main features into different chapters, building upon the information from previous chapters. You can see this by the chapter list, where in Chapter 4 we introduce and give an overview of Selenium RC, then in Chapter 5 we create our first Test Script then in Chapter 6 we execute that first Test Script. This approach allows for steady learning in chunks, so you do not get over-loaded with information and forget important information in the process, before you have had a chance to use it practically.

To this, the second prong, is to take a very detailed step-by-step approach through the given task of each chapter. This approach means we have a lot of screenshots (going step-by-step through a given task), you may feel you are able to "jump" pass some of the steps. If you are confident on doing that, that is great, but if you do get lost you can always go back.

1.5 Selenium RC Version

This book **Selenium By Example – Volume II: Selenium RC** uses the following configuration:

Selenium RC Version:	2.42.0.
Build Date:	3rd June 2014.
Platform:	Windows operating system.
Programming Language:	Java.

Although the configuration used in this book may be different to your configuration, e.g. you may use Linux and C#, the examples are still relevant and useful for you.

Chapter 2: What is Selenium RC?

Before we start to use Selenium RC we need to discuss what Selenium RC is and more importantly what it can do for you!

W hat is Selenium RC? This is the most important question within this book, and the answer to this question will drive a series of other questions, which you will be able to answer as you learn more about Selenium RC by going further through the book. But, before we can start to learn and use Selenium RC, we first need to discuss several topics around Selenium RC. The topics discussed in this chapter are:

- ✓ What Selenium RC is.
- ✓ What Selenium RC is capable of doing.
- ✓ What limitations exist around Selenium RC.
- ✓ How Selenium RC could help you.

2.1 What is Selenium RC

Selenium RC (also known as **Selenium Server 1.0**) (or to give it its' full name **Selenium Remote Control**) is a freeware Automated Testing software used to test Web-Based applications.

Selenium RC works by programming Test Scripts, in any one of several available languages: Java, C#, Ruby, Python, PHP, Perl, or JavaScript. These Test Scripts are a series of commands (the commands are known as **Selenese**).

You, as the Test Automation Engineer are responsible for writing the programming code (a mixture of one of the above languages and the Selenese commands) that perform the actions (for example clicking on a Button, entering text into a Text Box, selecting a value from a Combobox, etc.) which will test the functionality of your Web Application.

2.1.1 A brief history of the Selenium Project

Selenium was a project originally developed by Jason Huggins of ThoughtWorks in 2004. This was a collection of JavaScript rolled into a library, used to drive interactions with Web Pages. The decision was made to make Selenium available as open-source software via the Apache 2.0 license, and that library eventually became Selenium Core.

The Selenium Core library is the basic underlying functionality of both Selenium IDE (please see **Selenium By Example – Volume I: Selenium IDE** for more information on this) and Selenium RC (aka Selenium Remote Control aka Selenium Server 1.0).

Eventually, over time, Selenium Core library became Selenium Server 1.0, which became Selenium RC. Selenium RC was a ground-breaking Automated Testing tool, because no other product at that time allowed you to control a Web Browser from an array of programming languages.

2.1.2   Selenium Website
The Selenium projects have a whole community of individuals to help drive-on the project. The Selenium projects has documentation available on the main Selenium Website.

The main website for Selenium is available at the following URL:

http://seleniumhq.org/

The Selenium RC aspect of the Website is available using the URL:

http://seleniumhq.org/projects/remote-control/

The documentation for Selenium RC is available at the following URL:

http://seleniumhq.org/docs/05_selenium_rc.jsp

 You can find-out more information about Selenium RC at: http://seleniumhq.org/projects/remote-control/

2.2   What is Selenium RC capable of

Selenium RC allows you to program Test Scripts using a combination of one (of several programming languages: Java, C#, Ruby, Python, PHP, Perl, or JavaScript) and some built in Selenium functions (known as Selenese).

These Test Scripts are then compiled, and ran against the Selenium Server (Selenium RC), which uses a series of JavaScript libraries to perform the actions (e.g. clicking on a Button, entering text into a Text Box, selecting a value from a Combobox, etc.) against a Web Browser, to simulate a real user using the Web Application.

Selenium RC can run against all major Web Browsers that are JavaScript enabled. Below is a full list of Web Browsers that work with Selenium RC (assuming JavaScript is enabled in the Web Browser):

Web Browser	Works with Selenium RC
Chrome	Fully
Firefox all major Versions since version 3.6	Fully
Internet Explorer 11	Fully
Internet Explorer 10	Fully
Internet Explorer 9	Fully
Internet Explorer 8	Fully
Internet Explorer 7	Fully
Safari all major Versions since version 2	Fully

Opera all major Versions since Version 8	Fully
Others	Partially - if Web Browser supports JavaScript

 Your web-browser must support JavaScript for it to work with Selenium RC.

2.3 Limitations of Selenium RC

Selenium RC does have its' limitations. Selenium RC usage requires a level of knowledge of programming, and an understanding of one of the supported programming languages (Java, C#, Ruby, Python, PHP, Perl, or JavaScript), this makes the approach much more technical compared to record-and-playback approaches (such as Selenium IDE). That said, it is possible to use Selenium IDE to record some functionality and then export the code to be used in Selenium RC (please see **Selenium By Example – Volume I: Selenium IDE** for more information on this).

 You can get around the limitation of Selenium RC requiring programming experience, by using Selenium IDE to record the functionality and then exporting this into Selenium RC. Please see **Selenium By Example – Volume I: Selenium IDE** for more information on this.

Because it is a JavaScript based engine, as Web Browser have introduced more and more security restrictions around JavaScript code, and as Web Applications have become more powerful relying on new features within Web Browsers, Selenium RC has not been able to maintain its' original status of a ground-breaking tool.

That said Selenium RC is still an incredibly valuable Automated Testing tool, and experience and knowledge of Selenium RC continue to be highly sought-after skills to have.

2.4 How Selenium RC could help you

Selenium RC can aid you by allowing you to create (program) a series of Test Scripts to test the functionality of your Web Application. This can be particularly helpful when you face the following testing tasks:-

- You have the need to repeat test steps over and over.
- A large amount of test steps to test functionality.
- A large amount of combination needed to ensure test coverage of functionality.
- Functionality which will not change over-time, to ensure the execution of the Automated Test Script does not break.

Chapter 3: Installing Selenium RC

Before we start to use Selenium RC we need to firstly download and install Selenium RC.

The most important thing we can do when trying to make a decision on how useful a tool will be to help to test a Web Application, is to start using that tool to see how useful it could be.

To enable us to start using Selenium RC, we firstly need to download and install Selenium RC. This chapter will take you through the process of downloading and installing Selenium RC. The chapter concentrates on:

- ✓ System requirements for Selenium RC.
- ✓ Downloading Selenium RC.
- ✓ Installing Selenium RC.
- ✓ Running Selenium RC for the first time.

3.1 System Requirements

To be able to use Selenium RC you need the following installed and working on your computer:

- One of the following Operating Systems:

Operating System:
Windows
OS X
Linux
Solaris

- The following Java Runtime Framework Version:

Java Runtime Framework:
Java Version 1.5 (or later)

- You must also have one of the following Web Browsers installed:

Web Browser:
Chrome
Firefox (**version 3 or above**)
Internet Explorer (**version 7 or above**)
Safari (**version 2 or above**)
Opera (**version 8 or above**)

It is always best to upgrade to the latest version of your Web Browser.

3.2 Downloading Selenium RC

The first thing we need to do is download Selenium RC. Firstly, go to the Selenium Head Quarters (HQ) Website (http://www.seleniumhq.org/) as shown in Figure 3.1.

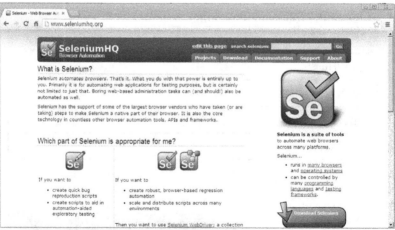

Figure 3.1. Selenium HQ Website.

Now click the **Download** Tab as shown in Figure 3.2.

What is Selenium?

Selenium automates browsers. That's it. What you do with that power is entirely up to you. Primarily it is for automating web applications for testing purposes, but is certainly not limited to just that. Boring web-based administration tasks can (and should!) also be automated as well.

Selenium has the support of some of the largest browser vendors who have taken (or are taking) steps to make Selenium a native part of their browser. It is also the core technology in countless other browser automation tools, APIs and frameworks.

Which part of Selenium is appropriate for me?

Figure 3.2. The Download Tab, highlighted with Red Border.

On the Download Page click the **Latest Version Number** Hyperlink (shown as 2.37.0 in Figure 3.3) of the Selenium RC Server section. This will cause the download to start happening, you may be prompted to confirm you want to keep the downloaded file (as shown in Figure 3.4). If this happens, please click the **Keep** Button (as shown in Figure 3.5).

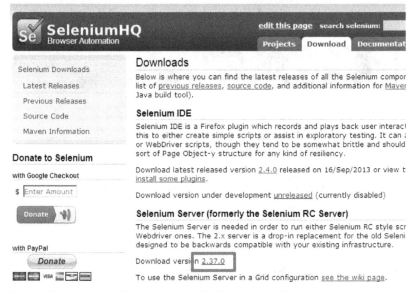

Figure 3.3. The Latest Version Number Hyperlink, highlighted with Red Border.

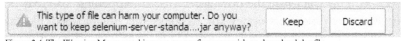

Figure 3.4. The Warning Message asking you to confirm you wish to download the file.

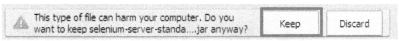

Figure 3.5. Click the Keep Button (highlighted in Red Border) to download the file.

After these steps, the file **Selenium-Server-Standalone-2.37.0.jar** (or whichever version is current) will be downloaded to your computer. In the next section we will install the file.

3.3 Installing Selenium RC

From the previous Section, Downloading Selenium RC, you will have downloaded the Selenium-Server-Standalone-2.37.0.jar (or whichever version is current) file to your computer. As the file is simply a Java Jar file it does not require any special installation routines.

Simply make a directory called **Selenium RC** on the root of your **C:** Drive. Copy the Selenium-Server-Standalone-2.37.0.jar (or whichever version is current) file into the C:\SeleniumRC Directory.

3.3.1 Renaming Selenium RC File

Please note that the version number of Selenium RC (2.37.0) will change with new builds. Unfortunately, the selenium-server-standalone file includes the version number (2.37.0).

This step is not necessary but is being done to ensure the commands and examples within this book are as generic as possible to ensure you can follow them.

Please rename the selenium-server-standalone-<version-number>.jar (selenium-server-standalone-2.37.0.jar) file to the following:

- **selenium-server-standalone.jar**

3.4 Running Selenium RC

Now let us confirm that Selenium RC runs correctly. Open a Windows Command Prompt and navigate to the C:\SeleniumRC\ Directory. Now enter the below command (as shown in Figure 3.6):

- **java –jar selenium-server-standalone.jar**

Figure 3.6. Windows Command Prompt with the **java -jar selenium-server-standalone.jar** command entered.

Now press the **Enter** Key to run the command, you should see the information shown in Figure 3.7 displayed.

Figure 3.7. Results of running the command in Figure 3.6.

If you see the results shown in Figure 3.7, this will confirm you have Selenium RC running correctly.

If you do not see the results shown in Figure 3.7, check your Java version and Path, check the Windows Path, and check the location Selenium is stored in.

Chapter 4: Selenium RC Structure

In this chapter of the book, we introduce the structure of Selenium RC, giving an overview of Selenium RC's structure and how it works.

N ow we have installed Selenium RC it is the right time to give an overview of the structure of Selenium RC. It is important to understand the structure of Selenium RC, and having an understanding of how Selenium RC works will aid with both learning Selenium RC and also ensure you use Selenium RC in the most suitable manner.

This chapter will cover the following items:

✓ An overview of the Selenium RC structure.
✓ How Selenium RC works.

4.1 Overview of the Selenium RC structure

The structure of Selenium RC is shown in Figure 4.1.

Starting at the bottom we have the Command Line (for running the Selenium RC Server), and also the Programming Code and Selenese (for running commands against the Selenium RC Server). This information is sent to the Selenium RC Server (which also returns results back to the Command Line). The Programming Code and Selenese are then sent to the Web Browsers (Chrome, Internet Explorer, Firefox, Opera, and Safari are shown here) – this is done via JavaScript calls from Selenium RC Server.

These JavaScript calls are sent to the Web Browser which perform the action on the Web Application that is being tested.

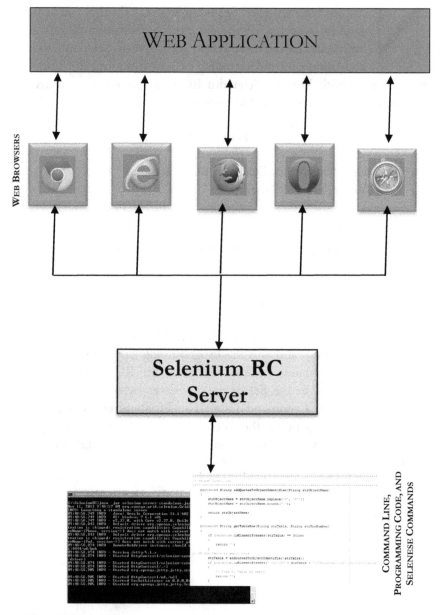

Figure 4.1. Selenium RC structure.

4.2 How Selenium RC works

Now we need to discuss how Selenium RC works, and how it does the tasks you see it do.

Let's first break-down into steps the various parts of the interaction:

- Commands to Selenium RC Server.
- Selenium RC Server to Web Browser (Selenium Core).
- Web Browser (Selenium Core) to Web Application.

4.2.1 Commands to Selenium RC Server

The first step is to send the Commands (which are made-up of the Command Line, Programming Code, and Selenese Commands) to the Selenium RC Server, as shown in Figure 4.2. This is done by the following:

The Programming Code and Selenese Commands are passed to the Selenium RC Server via the Command Line associated with the Selenium RC Server.

Figure 4.2. Commands sent to the Selenium RC Server via the Command Line.

4.2.2 Selenium RC Server to Web Browser (Selenium Core)

As mentioned earlier Selenium RC is made-up of a series of JavaScript Libraries, it is these JavaScript Libraries that interact with the Selenium Core element within the Web Browser, as shown in Figure 4.3.

Figure 4.3. Selenium RC Server sending JavaScript Commands to the Web Browser.

The interaction from Selenium RC Server to the Selenium Core element of the Web Browser is done by using JavaScript to send the Command to perform the actions performed on the Web Browser.

4.2.3 Web Browser (Selenium Code) to Web Application

The Selenium Core element of the Web Browser then simulates performing the actions the user would perform on the Web Browser (for example entering text into a Textbox; clicking a Button; etc.) against the Web Application, as shown in Figure 4.4.

Figure 4.4. Web Browser interacting with the Web Application (using the commands from Selenium Core).

Chapter 5: Creation of a Selenium RC Test Script

We are now ready to create our first Automated Test Script in Selenium RC.

U p until this point we have been discussing, installing, and understanding how Selenium RC works. Now we are at the point of getting our hands-dirty and starting to use Selenium RC.

This chapter will take you step-by-step through the creation of your first Selenium RC Test Script. This chapter covers:

✓ Creating a Selenium RC Test Script.

 Please note several steps (such as building a Java program and compiling a Java are outside of this book. If you need help on these please see documentation relating to Java.

5.1 Test Scenario
Let's set-out or Test Scenario for our first Selenium Test Script:

- Use Google to search for **BBC Weather** and confirm that the results contain **www.bbc.co.uk/weather/**.

5.2 Test Steps
Now let's break the Test Scenario down into a series of Test Steps:

1. Open Internet Explorer.
2. Load the Google Website.
3. Enter the search criteria **BBC Weather**.
4. Run the Google search.
5. Verify the results contains the text **www.bbc.co.uk/weather/**.

5.3 Create the Test Script
Now let's create the Test Script. Firstly, create a basic Java Class called **MyFirstTest**, include all the same package and imports as shown in Figure 5.1.

In the following examples all new code will be identified in **Bold** and *Italic* fonts.

```
package stepbystep.tests;

import com.thoughtworks.selenium.*;
import java.util.regex.Pattern;

public class MyFirstTest extends SeleneseTestCase
{
}
```

Figure 5.1. The Java Class **MyFirstTest**. New items highlighted in italic and bold font.

Figure 5.1, is the Java skeleton class of MyFirstTest, it is from the Package **stepbystep.tests**, and imports the following two Java Jar files **com.thoughworks.selenium** (all of the classes in that libraries) and **java.util.regex.Pattern** class. The MyFirstTest class extends the functionality in the default **SeleneseTestCase**.

To use Selenium RC you must import the **com.thoughworks.**selenium Java Library.

If you were to compile and run the Test Script at this point it would not actually do anything.

OK, now we need to define an object (of type **com.thoughworks.selenium.Selenium**) which we will call **selenium** this will be the Selenium RC Server instance we interact with (as shown in Figure 5.2).

```
package stepbystep.tests;

import com.thoughtworks.selenium.*;
import java.util.regex.Pattern;

public class MyFirstTest extends SeleneseTestCase
{
public static com.thoughtworks.selenium.Selenium selenium;
}
```

Figure 5.2. The **selenium** object (of type com.thoughtworks.selenium.Selenium). New items highlighted in italic and bold font.

You need to create an object of type **com.thoughworks.selenium**. This is the Selenium RC server you will be interacting with.

Let's now add a function **ConfigureSelenium** to setup and configure Selenium RC. Please see Figure 5.3. This configures the selenium object by setting some default settings for it (in this case for Internet Explorer).

```
package stepbystep.tests;

import com.thoughtworks.selenium.*;
import java.util.regex.Pattern;

public class MyFirstTest extends SeleneseTestCase
{
public static com.thoughtworks.selenium.Selenium selenium;

        public void ConfigureSelenium()
        throws Exception
        {
        selenium = new DefaultSelenium("localhost", 4444,
"*iehta", "http://www.google.co.uk");
        }
}
```

Figure 5.3. The **ConfigureSelenium** function. New items highlighted in italic and bold font.

You can get more information on the settings to configure Selenium RC with from the Selenium HQ (http://www.seleniumhq.org/).

Now let's add a new function **Test** which will actually do the Test Steps identified for this Test Scenario. The Test Function is shown in Figure 5.4.

The Test function has the following commands:

- selenium.open, which opens the www.google.co.uk website.

- selenium.type, which puts the value **BBC Weather** into the element called **q** (the Search Textbox).
- selenium.click, which clicks the button named "**btnG**" (the Search Button).
- selenium.waitForPageToLoad, which waits for the page to load or for a maximum of **30000** milliseconds (30 seconds).
- assertTrue(selenium.isTextPresent("www.bbc.co.uk/weather /")), which looks for the text **www.bbc.co.uk/weather/** and asserts whether the text is present on the page.

```
package stepbystep.tests;

import com.thoughtworks.selenium.*;
import java.util.regex.Pattern;

public class MyFirstTest extends SeleneseTestCase
{
public static com.thoughtworks.selenium.Selenium selenium;

    public void ConfigureSelenium()
    throws Exception
    {
    selenium = new DefaultSelenium("localhost", 4444,
"*iehta", "http://www.google.co.uk");
    }
    public void Test()
    throws Exception
    {
            selenium.open("http://www.google.co.uk/");
            selenium.type("q", "BBC Weather");
            selenium.click("btnG");
            selenium.waitForPageToLoad("30000");

            assertTrue(selenium.isTextPresent("www.bbc.co
    .uk/weather/"));
    }
}
```

Figure 5.4. The **Test** Function. New items highlighted in italic and bold font.

Now compile the program to ensure it does not have any syntax errors, and in the next chapter we will execute (run) the Test Script.

Chapter

6

Chapter 6: Executing a Selenium RC Test Script

We now execute the first Selenium RC Automation Test Script we created in the previous chapter.

I t is now time to execute the Selenium RC Test Script we created and compiled in the previous chapter (Chapter 5).

This chapter will take you step-by-step through the execution of your first Selenium RC Test Script. This chapter covers:

- ✓ Ways to execute a Selenium RC Test Script.
- ✓ Executing a Selenium RC Test Script.

 Please note several steps (such as building a Java program and compiling a Java are outside of this book. If you need help on these please see documentation relating to Java.

6.1 Ways to execute Test Script

There are three main ways to execute a Selenium RC Test Script:-

1. Command Line to run the Test Script.
2. Run the JAR File.
3. Via the Integrated Development Environment.

6.2 Command Line

The first method we will look at is to run your Selenium RC Test Script via a Command Line command. This can be simply achieved by completing the following steps:-

1. Compile your Java code into a JAR File. **If you need help to do this please see your Java Documentation.**
2. Run a simple Command Line to load both Selenium RC and your JAR File.

The command to run Selenium RC and your JAR File is given below:

- **java –jar selenium-server-standalone.jar <JAR File>**

If we assume that your JAR File is named **TestScript.jar**, the command you would need to enter would be:-

- **java –jar selenium-server-standalone.jar TestScript.jar**

This command will do the following:-

1. Load the Selenium RC Server (**selenium-server-standalone.jar**).
2. Run your Test Script (**TestScript.jar**).

6.3 Run JAR File

The second method we will look at is to run your Selenium RC Test Script via running your JAR File. This can be simply achieved by completing the following steps:-

1. Compile your Java code into a JAR File. **If you need help to do this please see your Java Documentation.**
2. Run a simple Command Line to load Selenium RC.
3. Run your JAR File.

As you can see this very similar to the first method to run your Test Script, but this time there is an additional step involved. This method does incur an additional step but may be more familiar to people who have previously ran Java code. The command to run Selenium RC is:

- **java –jar selenium-server-standalone.jar**

The command to run your JAR File is given below:

- **java –jar <JAR File>**

If we assume that your JAR File is named **TestScript.jar**, the command you would need to enter would be:-

- **java –jar TestScript.jar**

This command will do the following:-

1. Load the Selenium RC Server (**selenium-server-standalone.jar**).
2. Run your Test Script (**TestScript.jar**).

6.4 Run in IDE

The third method we will look at is to run your Selenium RC Test Script directly via your Integrated Development Environment. This method would use an option like Build or Execute within the Integrated Development Environment. This option will Build your JAR File and then run it.

Bear-in-mind that you will need to have started Selenium RC, so it is running. The command to run Selenium RC is:

- **java –jar selenium-server-standalone.jar**

6.5 Run Selenium RC Server

Whichever method you use to run your Test Script the most important step is to ensure that the Selenium RC Server is running before you run your Test Script. As I am sure you know the command to run Selenium RC is:

- **java –jar selenium-server-standalone.jar**

 Ensure you have started Selenium RC, and that it is running before running your Test Scripts.

Failure, to run the Selenium RC Server **before** you run your Test Script will result in your Test Script failing.

6.6 Which Method?

Which method you choose to run your Test Script should be based purely on which you find easiest/most convenient. None of the methods offer any benefit over the others, and equally none of the methods offer any drawbacks.

So the choice comes down to your personal preference, what is easiest/most convenient/best for you, what is technically most suitable, and also what is configured in your setup.

Chapter

7

Chapter 7: Advanced Selenium RC Test Scripts

Now is time to try add some of the more advanced concepts to the Selenium RC Test Script.

I n Chapter 5 we create a Selenium RC Test Script, and then

discussed executing this in Chapter 6. This chapter, we will enhance the Selenium RC Test Script by adding some additional features to this Test Script.

This chapter will cover the following items:-

- ✓ Additional useful Selenium RC functions.
- ✓ Standard coding techniques.
- ✓ Using multiple calls to Selenium RC functions.

7.1 Useful Selenium RC Functions

The full list of Selenium RC Functions is given in Appendix A, but here we will go through a list of the functions you will find more useful, during the development of your Test Scripts.

The list of Selenium RC Functions we will cover are:-

- Click
- ClickAt
- Focus
- Highlight
- KeyDown
- MouseDownAt
- Type

7.1.1 Click

The **Click** function is probably one of the Selenium RC Functions you will use most often when testing via Selenium RC. The Click function is used to allow Selenium RC to click on an object (for example a Button, a Textbox, an Image, etc.)

The Click function can be used against any Web Page element (object), regardless of whether it triggers that Web Page element to do anything or not, e.g. you can use the Click function to click on an Image even-though the clicking on the Image will not do anything.

As well as the obvious usage of the Click function, where you click a Web Page element to trigger an action, e.g. clicking a Button to save a page, it is also very useful in the following situations:-

- To ensure a Web Page element is selected.
- To ensure a Web Page element has focus.

The syntax for the Click function is shown below, and an example of using the Click functionality to click on the button **btnSave** is shown in Figure 7.1.

- Selenium.click(*element name*)

```
selenium.click("btnSave");
```

Figure 7.1. The **Click** function.

7.1.2 ClickAt

The **ClickAt** function is an extremely useful Selenium RC Function, particvularly when the Click Function (Section 7.1.1) does not work. The ClickAt function is used to allow Selenium RC to click at a certain location on an object (for example a certain Button, a Textbox, an Image, etc.)

The ClickAt function can be used against any Web Page element, regardless of whether it triggers that Web Page element to do something or not, e.g. you can use the ClickAt function to click on an Image even-though the clicking on the Image will not do anything.

As well as the obvious usage of the ClickAt function, where you click a Web Page element to trigger an action, e.g. clicking a Button to save a page, it is also very useful in the following situations:-

- To ensure a Web Page element is selected.
- To ensure a Web Page element has focus.

The ClickAt function requires both the Web Page element to click on and the position (in x, y format) from the positon of the Web Page element (top left position of the Web Page element) to click at.

The syntax for the ClickAt function is shown below, and an example of clicking on the button **btnOpen** at the location of 10 pixels from the left and 20 pixels from the top, is shown in Figure 7.2.

- Selenium.clickAt(*element name, position string*)

```
selenium.click("btnOpen", "10, 20");
```

Figure 7.2. The **ClickAt** function. Clicking 10 pixels into and 20 pixels down from the top-left of the btnOpen Web Page element.

7.1.3 Focus

The **Focus** function is used to set a Web Page element to have focus. The function can be used against any Web Page element that can gain focus, and is extremely useful to ensure a Web Page element can accept input e.g. the selenium type command (Section 7.1.7) to type text.

The syntax for the Focus function is shown below, and an example of using the Focus Function on the **txtFirstname** is shown in Figure 7.3.

- Selenium.focus(*element name*)

```
selenium.focus(txtFirstname);
```

Figure 7.3. The **Focus** function.

7.1.4 Highlight

The **Highlight** function is probably one of the most useful Selenium RC Functions to usewhen you are debugging a Test Script.

The Highlight function is used to highlight (in a bright yellow colour) the Web Page element. Why is this so useful? When you are debugging a Test Script it is useful for a variety of reasons:-

- To identify a Web Page element.
- To work-out whether a Web Page element is visible/usable.

The syntax for the Highlight function is shown below, and an example of using the Highlight Function on the button **btnClose** is shown in Figure 7.4.

- Selenium.highlight(*element name*)

```
selenium.highlight(btnClose);
```

Figure 7.4. The **Highlight** function.

7.1.5 KeyDown

The **KeyDown** function is useful for when you find that you need a work-around to a particular situation. Selenium provides the type function (see Section 7.1.7) which is used to enter input via the keyboard. However, in practice you will experience times where the type function does not work. In these instances the KeyDown function will provide a solution. This offers particular value when using certain keys: Arrow Cursor; Shift; Control; Enter; etc.

The syntax for the KeyDown function is shown below, and an example using the KeyDown to send the Down Arrow Cursor Key is shown in Figure 7.5.

- Selenium.click(*Key*)

```
selenium.keyDown(Keys.DOWN);
```

Figure 7.5. The **KeyDown** function.

7.1.6 MouseDownAt

The **MouseDownAt** function is probably one of the Selenium RC Functions you will use most often when testing using Selenium RC. The MouseDownAt function is used to allow Selenium RC to put down the Mouse Cursor at a certain location on an object (for example a Button, a Textbox, an Image, etc.)

As well as the obvious usage of the MouseDownAt function, where you click a Web Page element to trigger an action, e.g. clicking a Button to save a page, it is also very useful in the following situations:-

- To ensure a Web Page element is selected.
- To ensure a Web Page element has focus.
- To trigger any sub-menus; drop-downs; etc.

The MouseDownAt function requires both the Web Page element to click on at the position (in x, y format) from the positon of the Web Page element (top left position of the Web Page element).

The syntax for the MouseDownAt function is shown below, and an example of sending the MouseDownAt Call (at 15 Pixels from the left, and 30 Pixels from the Top) on the image **imgLogo** is shown in Figure 7.6.

- Selenium.mouseDownAt(*element name, position string*)

```
selenium.mouseDownAt("imgLogo", "15, 30");
```

Figure 7.6 The **MouseDownAt** function. Clicking 15 pixels into and 30 pixels down from the top-left of the imgLogo Web Page element.

7.1.7 Type

The **Type** function is one of the Selenium RC Functions you will use to allow you to enter data into an input Web Page element.

The Type function can be used against any Web Page element, regardless of whether it expects input or not. This may seem a little strange, but it does allow you (with the combination of other Selenium RC functions) to send not just standard values (a-z;0-9; etc.) but also special values (Cursors; Alt; Control; Enter; etc.) Therefore you can use it to select an item; enter text; select items in a drop-down; etc.

The syntax for the Type function is shown below, and an example of typing into the textbox **txtName** is shown in Figure 7.7.

- Selenium.type(*element name, value*)

```
selenium.type("txtName", "John Smith");
```

Figure 7.7. The **Type** function.

7.2 Standard Coding Techniques

As well as the Selenium RC Functions, to be able to successful implement automated testing with Selenium RC it is necessary to learn several standard coding techniques.

These standard coding techniques will offer great value to your automated test scripts, including: offering enhanced functionality; making them more reliable; making them more re-usable; making them faster to write and execute.

The list of Standard Coding Techniques we will cover are:-

- Variables
- Functions
- If statements
- Loop statements

7.2.1 Variables

Variables are one of the most useful tools in development. A Variable consists of the following pieces of information:-

- Variable Name.

- Type.
- Data.

The **Variable Name** is used to uniquely identify the Variable's data, and provides a way of referencing that data during usage. The **Type** determines the data that the Variable will be allowed to store.

Java offers the following Basic Data Types (other programming languages will offer similar Basic Data Types):-

- **Byte**. For storing integer byte values between -128 and 1211.
- **Short**. A 16-bit integer value between -32768 and 32767.
- **Int**. A 32-bit signed integer value between - 2,147,483,648 and 2,147,483,647.
- **Long**. A 64-bit signed integer, allowing values between - 9,223,372,036,854,775,808 and 9,223,372,036,854,775,807.
- **Float**. A 32-bit single-precision floating point number.
- **Double**. A 64-bit double-precision floating point number.
- **Boolean**. Represents one bit of data, with two possible values: true and false.
- **Char**. A 16-bit Unicode character used to store letters.

To this Java (and other programming languages) also offers Reference Data Types, which are constructions of multiple Basic Data Types, common example is **String** which is a collection of **Char** items.

Now let's look at the syntax of declaring a Variable without setting it's data (Figure 7.8):-

```
<Data Type> <Variable Name>;
```

Figure 7.8. Syntax of declaring a Variable without setting the data.

Let's take a look at an example of declaring a Variable (without setting it's data) for an **Int** item (Figure 7.9):-

```
int myvariable;
```

Figure 7.9. Declaring a variable.

Figure 7.9, shows the declaring of an **int** Type Variable with the Variable Name of **myvariable**.

Let's look at the syntax of declaring a Variable with setting it's data (Figure 7.10):-

```
<Data Type> <Variable Name> = <Data>;
```

Figure 7.10. Syntax of declaring a Variable with setting the data.

Let's take a look at an example of declaring a Variable (with setting it's data) for an **Char** item (Figure 7.11):-

```
char mysecondvariable = 'a';
```

Figure 7.11. Declaring a variable.

Figure 7.11, shows the declaring of an **char** Type Variable with the Variable Name of **mysecondvariable**, setting it's Data to be **a**. Note that as this is a char value we need to put the value in single quotes.
The **Type** function is one of the Selenium RC Functions you will use most often, as it allows you to enter data into an input Web Page element.

7.2.2 Functions

Functions are a way of grouping code into modules, they provide a means of grouping code together to aid splitting-off unrelated bits of code and also aiding the re-usability of code.

7.2.3 If Statements

If Statements are conditional statements which can be used to get one or another piece of code executed. You can have basic If statements (which will be executed if the condition is true); If-Else Statements (which will execute the If when the condition is true, otherwise execute the Else). If statements can be nested inside other If statements.

7.2.4 Loop Statements

Loop Statements allow you to loop the same code several times, and are again controlled by whether the condition evaluates to true or not. Some of the available Loop Statements are: For Loops; While Loops; Do-While Loops.

Chapter

8

Chapter 8: Interacting with Web Elements

Let's start to identify the necessary Selenium RC functions we need to use to be able to interact with various Web Page Elements

N ow we have created a Test Script in Selenium RC, it is the

right time to start to think about the Selenium RC functions you will need to use to be able to interact with the various Web Page Elements you find on most Web Applications, we will cover the following:

✓ The correct Selenium RC function or functions to be able to use a Web Page Element.

8.1 Web Element Overview

Modern Web Applications use a variety of Web Page Elements to allow users to interact with the Web Application. These Web Page Elements can range from standard elements such as: **Textboxes, Comboboxes, Buttons**, etc. to standard HTML elements, such as **Panels, Frames**, etc., to more specific elements used less frequently, for example such as **Numeric Range Boxes, Slider Bars**, etc.

This chapter will cover interacting and using the following Web Page Elements:

- Alert Dialog
- Button.
- Checkbox.
- Combobox.
- Frame.
- Image.
- Image Button.

- Label.
- Listbox.
- Numeric Range Textbox.
- Panel.
- Password Textbox.
- Radio Button.
- Sliderbar.
- Textbox.

8.1.1 Alert Dialog

To interact and use an **Alert Dialog** you will use the following Selenium RC function(s):

- **SelectWindow**   *To select the window*
- **Click**   *To click on a button or object*

8.1.2 Button

To interact and use a **Button** you will use the following Selenium RC function(s):

- **Click**   *To click on a button*
- **ClickAt**   *To click on a button at a certain location*
- **MouseDownAt**   *To perform MouseDown (Click) on a button at a certain location*

8.1.3 Checkbox

To interact and use a **Checkbox** you will use the following Selenium RC function(s):

- **Click**   *To click on a button*
- **ClickAt**   *To click on a button at a certain location*

- **MouseDownAt**   *To perform MouseDown (Click) on a button at a certain location*
- **DoubleClick**   *To Double-Click the item.*

8.1.4 Combobox
To interact and use a **Combobox** you will use the following Selenium RC function(s):

8.1.5 Frame
To interact and use a **Frame** you will use the following Selenium RC function(s):

- **Click**   *To click the Frame so it has focus.*

8.1.6 Image
To interact and use a **Image** you will use the following Selenium RC function(s):

- **Click**   *To click on the Image*
- **ClickAt**   *To click on the Image at a certain location*
- **MouseDownAt**   *To perform MouseDown (Click) on a button at a certain location*

8.1.7 Imagebutton
To interact and use an **Imagebutton** you will use the following Selenium RC function(s):

- **Click**   *To click on a button*
- **ClickAt**   *To click on a button at a certain location*
- **MouseDownAt**   *To perform MouseDown (Click) on a button at a certain location*

8.1.8 Label

To interact and use a **Label** you will use the following Selenium RC function(s):

- **IsElementPresent**   *Confirm the Element is on the Page.*
- **GetText**   *Get the Text of the Element*
- **IsTextPresent**   *Checks whole Page for the Text.*

8.1.9 Listbox

To interact and use a **Listbox** you will use the following Selenium RC function(s):

- **Click**   *To click on a button*
- **ClickAt**   *To click on a button at a certain location*
- **MouseDownAt**   *To perform MouseDown (Click) on a button at a certain location*

8.1.10 Numeric Range Textbox

To interact and use a **Numeric Range Textbox** you will use the following Selenium RC function(s):

- **Type**   *To "type" the text*

8.1.11 Panel

To interact and use a **Panel** you will use the following Selenium RC function(s):

- **Click**   *To click the Panel so it has focus.*

8.1.12 Password Textbox

To interact and use a **Password Textbox** you will use the following Selenium RC function(s):

- **Type**   *To "type" the text*

8.1.13 Radio Button

To interact and use a **Radio Button** you will use the following Selenium RC function(s):

- **Click**   *To click on a button*
- **ClickAt**   *To click on a button at a certain location*
- **MouseDownAt**   *To perform MouseDown (Click) on a button at a certain location*

8.1.14 Sliderbar

To interact and use a **Sliderbar** you will use the following Selenium RC function(s):

- **Click**   *To click on a button*
- **ClickAt**   *To click on a button at a certain location*
- **MouseDownAt**   *To perform MouseDown (Click) on a button at a certain location*

8.1.15 Textbox

To interact and use a **Textbox** you will use the following Selenium RC function(s):

- **Type**   *To "type" the text*

Chapter 9: Identifying Web Elements

Now is the time to discuss the ways and challenges of identifying Web Elements

N ow we have created and enhanced a Test Script in

Selenium RC, it is worth spending a little time discussing how you can identify Web Page Elements and some of the challenges faced when trying to identify Web Page Elements. This chapter will cover:

✓ Identifying Web Elements.
✓ Challenges identifying Web Elements.
✓ Tips to select a Web Element.

9.1 Identifying Web Elements

From the Automation Tools perspective, identifying Web Elements is a case of going through the Source Code for the Web Page (from top-to-bottom) and will select the first item (Web Element) with the given name.

Selenium RC allows you to select Web Elements via several means:

- Identifier
- Id
- Name
- Link
- DOM
- CSS
- XPath

This offers a lot of options to identifying Web Elements on the Page of the Web Application you are testing using Selenium RC.

Although, this may seem like over-kill it is a necessity, as you will find that Selenium RC will fail to identify Web Elements with one method, but identify the Web Element with another.

9.1.1 Identifier

The Identifier method works with both the **id** and **name** attributes of HTMLs tags of a Web Element. An example of this is shown in Figure 9.1 using the name attribute on the HTML Element <input name="username" type="text"/>:-

```
identifier=username
```

Figure 9.1. Using the Identifier method on the **name** attribute.

Figure 9.2 using the id attribute on the HTML Element <input id="user_password" type="password"/>:-

```
identifier=user_password
```

Figure 9.2. Using the Identifier method on the **id** attribute.

The Identifier method does not rely on the structure of the page and to a certain level will continue to work when Web Elements are changed. The biggest problem of the Identifier method is it may match several items, if they have the same name or id attributes.

9.1.2 Id

The Id method works with both the **id** attribute of HTMLs tags of a Web Element. An example of this is shown in Figure 9.3 using HTML Element <label id="title" />:-

```
Id=title
```

Figure 9.3. Using the Id method.

The Id method does relies on the Id of each Web Element being unique. The biggest problems of the Id method are if the Ids prove to not be unique or change, as then the Web Element will not be found.

9.1.3 Name

The Name method works with both the **name** attribute of HTMLs tags of a Web Element. An example of this is shown in Figure 9.4 using HTML Element <button type="button" name="save" />:-

```
name=save
```

Figure 9.4. Using the Name method.

The Name method does relies on the Nameof each Web Element being unique, if there are two Web Elements with the Name **Save** Selenium RC will always return the first. This method is also impacted to the Name being changed.

9.1.4 Link

The Link method works with identifying the text of Links within the HTMLs tags of a Web Element. An example of this is shown in Figure 9.5:-

```
link=Click here to move to the next page
```

Figure 9.5. Using the Link method.

The Link method is useful for testing the navigation Web Elements (Links, etc.) This method is reliant on the Text being both unique and not changing.

9.1.5 DOM

The DOM method works with identifying the Web Element via the DOM (Document Object Model) for the Web Page. An example of this is shown in Figure 9.6:-

```
dom=document.div[0].button[3]
```

Figure 9.6. Using the DOM method.

The DOM allows you to use JavaScript for dynamic locators, but is reliant on the structure of the Web Page. When the Web Page structure changes the method will fail.

9.1.6 CSS

The CSS method works with identifying the Web Element via the CSS (Cascading Style Sheet) for the Web Page. An example of this is shown in Figure 9.7:-

```
css=div[id=save]
```

Figure 9.7. Using the CSS method.

The CSS allows you to select Web Elements from the surrounding items to the Web Element, and is fast at identifying Web Elements. However, this method is very complex requiring a lot of technical abilities to identify Web Elements.

9.1.7 XPath

The XPath method allows you to navigate via the DOM to identify the Web Element. An example of this is shown in Figure 9.8:-

```
xpath=//button[@value="Save"]
```

Figure 9.8. Using the Xpath method.

The XPath allows you to precise identify Web Elements on a Web Page. However, this method is very complex requiring a lot of technical abilities to identify Web Elements and quite slow at identifying Web Elements.

9.2 Challenges identifying Web Elements

The most common challenges you experience when trying to identify Web Elements are:

- Web Elements not being unique.
- Web Elements changing.
- Web Pages changing.

When Web Elements are not unique, Selenium RC will always return the first Web Element with that Name/Id/etc. in the DOM. This may or may not be the actual Web Element you wish to use.

When Web Elements change, for example the Id changes each time the software is built, Selenium RC will end-up accessing a completely different Web Element.

When Web Pages change, you will find that some Web Elements will stop being identified.

9.3 Tips to select a Web Element

Depending on the approach you use plan to use (either **Structure** or **Attribute** based) will determine which method to use.

If you are using Structure method, you will need to use one of the following:-

- CSS
- DOM
- XPath

If you are using an Attribute method to identify Web Elements, you can use one of the following:-

- CSS
- Id
- Identifier
- Link
- Name

Some tips to help identify a Web Element via Selenium RC are:-

- Choose a method which is unique.
- Choose a method which is unlikely to change.
- If the Web Application uses Panels and Tabs, then click on the Panel and Tab before using the intended Web Element.
- Use the **Highlight** function in Selenium RC to help to identify which Web Element is selected.

- Use the **IsElementPresent** function in Selenium RC to confirm the Web Element exists from Selenium RC's point-of-view.
- Although hard to learn, XPath will allow you to navigate to the precise Web Element.

This list of tips have been gained from my many years of using Automated Testing Software and Selenium RC, you may find unique challenges which you will need to work around.

Chapter 10: Automated Test Script Structure

Let us discuss the correct structure and approach to creating Automated Test Scripts.

I t is time to discuss a good approach to creating Automated Test

Scripts and also the correct structure for an Automated Test Script to have. This is very important, as it will ensure that the Automated Test Scripts you create offer good value to your testing; produce the correct results; offer good quality of testing; improve testing coverage; and most importantly identify defects. The chapter will discuss the following:

✓ Correct approach to creating Automated Test Scripts.
✓ Correct structure for Automated Test Scripts.

10.1 Introduction

I thought long-and-hard on whether to include this chapter in the book, as the chapter is trying to tell you *what to do* and *how to do it!* You and your company will have testing processes and structures, so who am I to suggest you do *this task this way*. But in the end I thought it best to input, give you some advice from my experience which will hopefully help you; if it does not or you better procedures then the only thing lost is the time it has taken you to read this chapter.

Like all Test Scripts, Test Scripts for Automated Testing need to be done in a way to offer most value to the overall Testing approach. The aim of the Test Script (Manual or Automated is to find the most defects available; test in the most cost-effective way; and ensure the best quality software.)

10.2 Approach for Automated Test Scripts

Automated Test Scripts need to be approach in a slight more complex way to normal Test Script, this is due to the fact that the Automated Testing Software (Selenium RC) does not think, the Automated Testing Software just does what you tell it to do. Therefore your Automated Test Scripts need to tell the Automated Test Scripts the following:-

1. What to do.
2. How to do it.

The approach to creating an Automated Test Script should be as Figure 10.1 shows.

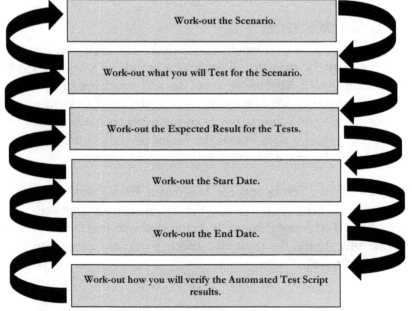

Figure 10.1. Automated Test Script recommended approach.

As you can see from Figure 10.1, each of the steps inter-relates to the other steps. The output from one could be either the input to the next step or result in a change to the previous step. The whole approach is iterative.

10.3 Structure for Automated Test Scripts

Automated Test Scripts need to have a certain structure to ensure that they do all the necessary testing. Some of this is done instinctively by a Human performing manual testing, but we are writing Test Scripts for Automated Testing Software (Selenium RC), and that does not do anything instinctively. Figure 10.2 shows the structure to use when creating an Automated Test Script.

Structure for an Automated Test Script:

1. Known start.
2. Navigate to the Web Page.
3. Verify the Web Page Elements.
4. Verify the Web Page Data.
5. Test the Web Page Functionality.
6. Navigate away from the Web Page.
7. Navigate back to the Web Page.
8. Verify the Web Page Elements.
9. Verify the Web Page Data.
10. Verify the Web Page Data against expected Data.

Figure 10.2. Automated Test Script recommended structure

Notice that recommended Automated Test Script Structure is using Step 1 (Known start) to ensure we know what the initial data (user login; test data; etc.) is correct; next Steps 2-4 take you to the Web Page, verifies it's Elements (Textboxes are showing; etc.), and verifies the initial data for the Web Page; Step 5 then performs the actual steps to test the Web Page functionality; Steps 6-9, then navigate away from and then back to the page (to ensure the data is not cached), re-confirms the Web Page Elements and Data (this is verifying the Functional Testing worked). Finally, Step 10, checks the Web Page Data against the Expected Data, this validates your Automation Test Script, for example if the Automated Test Script missed/was incorrect on one step, you will find the result is not as expected so know there is a problem.

Chapter 11: Automation Framework discussion

Now is time to have a discussion of the various types of Automation Framework available.

N ow we have created, executed (ran), and enhanced a Test

Script in Selenium RC, it is time to think about building an Automation Framework to use against Selenium RC. This chapter will start to discuss the various Automation Framework types that exist and give pros and cons for each, the discussion will include:

- ✓ How an Automation Framework works.
- ✓ Benefits and drawbacks of an Automation Framework.
- ✓ The different types of Automation Frameworks.
- ✓ Which Automation Framework is best for which situation?

11.1 Automation Frameworks Overview

Automation Frameworks are affectively wrappers which sit between Test Scripts and the Automation Testing Tool. As you will see in the following sections, the various approaches to Automation Frameworks achieve this wrapper in different ways but overall the principle is the same for all the Automation Framework approaches. Figure 11.1 shows the basic concept of an Automation Framework.

At the very highest level the Automation Framework works by "sitting" between the Test Scripts code and the Automation Tool (Selenium RC). We then write automation to use the Automation Framework rather than using the Automation Tool.

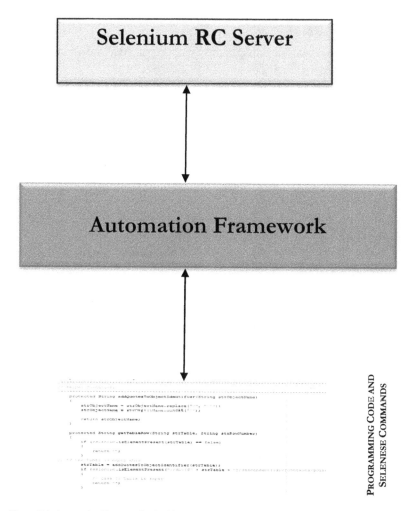

Figure 11.1. Automation Framework principle.

This indirection allows several advantages and some disadvantages, which will be discussed in the next section. Overall the advantages of using an Automation Framework far out-weigh the disadvantages.

11.2 Advantages of using a Framework

There can be several advantages when you use an Automation Frameworks, these include:-

- Future Proofing.
- Ease of use.
- Flexibility of approach.

An Automation Framework can help to future proof your automation by means of placing a layer between the Test Script and the Automation Tool, as you will see with some of the Automation Framework approaches you can effectively have a Command in the Test Script that the Automation Framework translates into a command for the Automation Tool, so if you change the Automation Tool (i.e. go from Selenium RC to Telerik Web UI) you only have to alter the Automation Framework (i.e. the translation aspect), all the Test Scripts will then still work.

Automation Frameworks can be easier to use, in terms of you can tailor the Automation Framework to the technical needs of your Technical capabilities. This can also make them more flexible to your needs.

11.3 Dis-advantages of using a Framework

Automation Frameworks can have several dis-advantages, including:-

- More time-consuming to develop.
- Slower to execute.
- More complex to create.
- More complex to debug.

11.4 Types of Automation Framework

There are several types of Automation Framework available to use as Automation Frameworks:-

- Module Automation Framework.
- Data-Driven Automation Framework.
- Key Word Driven Automation Framework
- Page Object Automation Framework.

11.5 Module Automation Framework

The Module Automation Framework is built around the concept of building "Modules" around the functionality of the software. You encapsulate discreet functionality into modules which you then "join" together to test the functionality of the software. Figure 11.2 shows an overview of a Module Automation Framework.

As an example, let's say you have three discreet chunks of functionality in the system:-

1. Login.
2. Create New User.
3. Delete User.

Each of these bits of functionality becomes a module, for example:-

- ModuleA_Login.
- ModuleB_CreateUser.
- ModuleC_DeleteUser.

You can then join the Modules together to test the coverage of the functionality, for example:-

- To test you can create and use a User, you could join the following:

  o ModuleA_Login — *Login as the user to create another user.*
  o ModuleB_CreateUser - *Create the new user.*
  o ModuleA_Login - *Login as the newly created user.*

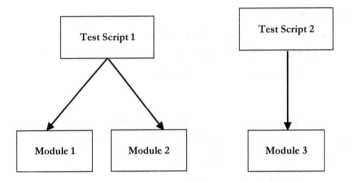

Figure 11.2. Module Automation Framework.

Some of the advantages of using the Module Automation approach include:-

- It will be faster to execute.
- The approach is very "clean", mapping modules to functionality in the software, which will help in planning the building of the Automation Framework; help identify what aspects of the Automation Framework which will need to be modified when the software's functionality is changed; ensure problems with the Automation Framework are localized to functionality.
- Enable multiple people to develop the Automation Framework in isolation as each Module can be created in isolation of the other Modules.

However, the Module Automation approach does have some drawbacks:-

- The Automation Framework is very tied to the software being tested, it is not flexible and cannot be used on other software.
- The approach is heavily dependent on developing code and this means the skill-set needed is very technical.
- As the Modules are isolated and self-contained including the data they use, simple changes to the software can require a lot of change for the Automation Framework.

11.6 Data Driven Automation Framework

A Data Driven Automation Framework is where the test input and the expected output results are stored in a separate data file so that a single driver script can execute all the test cases with multiple sets of data. This is shown in Figure 11.3.

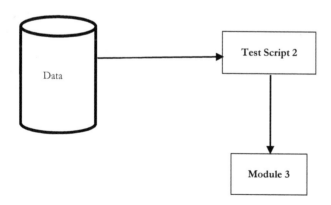

Figure 11.3. Data Driven Automation Framework.

Some of the advantages of the Data Driven Automation Framework are:-

- A reduced number of overall test scripts needed to implement all the test cases.
- Less amount of code is required to generate all the test cases.
- The test data can be created before test implementation is ready or even.

Some of the disadvantages include:-

- The Test Scripts are very static, offering little-to-no flexibility. This will mean if you cannot re-use the Data in other Test Scripts.
- Basic changes to the software will result in the Test Scripts and Data becoming out-of-date and requiring being re-done.

11.7 Keyword Driven Automation Framework

A Keyword Driven Automation Framework is where the Test Script is made-up of a series of Keywords (commands) which are interpreted and turned into that are sent to the Automation Testing Tool and actioned against the software being tested. Effectively there is a step where the Test Script Command (Keyword) is translated into the Automation Testing Tool command, as shown in Figure 11.4.

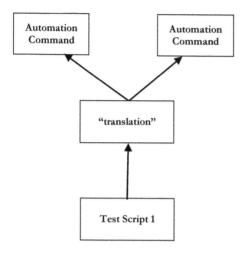

Figure 11.4. Keyword Automation Framework.

Example of a Keyword Driven Test Script, as shown in Figure 11.5:

Command	Object	Value
EnterText	txtName	Steven
Click	btnLogin	

Figure 11.5. Example Test Script for Keyword Automation Framework.

Some of the advantages of the Keyword Driven Framework are:-

- Automation expertise is not required to maintain or create a new Test Scripts.
- Keywords are reused across multiple Test Scripts (or even different software).
- Data can be kept separate (to a limited extent).

- You can future-proof yourself by making it Automation Tool independent.

Some of the disadvantages are:-

- The main problem is that this requires a more technically complicated framework to be developed.
- With the keyword driven approach the Test Scripts are longer and more complex, taking more time to create and maintain.

11.8 Page Object Automation Framework

A Page Object Automation Framework is similar in concept to Object Orientated Development (in the software development world), where you identify all the Object (Textboxes, Buttons, etc.) and the actions you want to perform on them for one particular page.

Some of the advantages of the Keyword Driven Framework are:-

- It is more Object Orientated that other approaches, resulting in commands and data encapsulated together.
- It allows you to identify impacts and changes to a page more easily.

Some of the disadvantages are:-

- It can be technical difficult to implement, as it resumes more technically development experience.
- Changes to a Page can have a wide impact, breaking large parts of the Automation Framework.

11.9 Hybrid Automation Framework

Hybrid Automation Frameworks exist, which are hybrids of two or more of standard Automation Frameworks. These tend to be very specific and very complex in terms of developing them.

11.10 Choice of Automation Framework

The Automation Framework you choose to use is dependent on the software you intend to test, there is no hard-and-fast rule to say that a particular Automation Framework is best suited for a particular piece of software, but there are some guidelines on what is appropriate and in what situations.

The choice you make for which Automation Framework you use should be based on answers to the following questions:-

1. **Specific/Generic**: Whether this is a specific Automation Framework for one piece of software or it needs to be a generic Automation Framework for several pieces of software.
2. **Tool Dependency**: How likely it is for the Automation Tool will need to be replaced by a new Automation Tool in the future.
3. **Software Complexity**: The needs of the software you are testing, in terms of how complex the software being tested is.
4. **Technical Capabilities**: The technical capabilities of the resources you have to build the Automation Framework.

The below matrix (Figure 11.6) gives some guidance on the choice of Automation Framework depending on the answer to **Question 1** above:-

Framework	Framework needs to be Specific?	Framework needs to be Generic?
Module	Very Suitable	Less Suitable
Data Driven	Very Suitable	Less Suitable
Keyword Driven	Very Suitable	Very Suitable
Page Object	Very Suitable	Less Suitable

Figure 11.6. Matrix for Answers to Question 1.

The below matrix (Figure 11.7) gives some guidance on the choice of Automation Framework depending on the answer to **Question 2** above:-

Framework	Tool will not be replaced?	Tool may need to be replaced?
Module	Very Suitable	Less Suitable
Data Driven	Very Suitable	Less Suitable
Keyword Driven	Very Suitable	Somewhat Suitable
Page Object	Very Suitable	Somewhat Suitable

Figure 11.7. Matrix for Answers to Question 2.

The below matrix (Figure 11.8) gives some guidance on the choice of Automation Framework depending on the answer to **Question 3** above:-

Framework	Software very complex?	Software less complex?

Module	Very Suitable	Very Suitable
Data Driven	Very Suitable	Very Suitable
Keyword Driven	Less Suitable	Very Suitable
Page Object	Less Suitable	Very Suitable

Figure 11.8. Matrix for Answers to Question 3.

The below matrix (Figure 11.9) gives some guidance on the choice of Automation Framework depending on the answer to **Question 4** above:-

Framework	High technical capabilities	Low technical capabilities
Module	Very Suitable	Less Suitable
Data Driven	Very Suitable	Less Suitable
Keyword Driven	Very Suitable	Somewhat Suitable
Page Object	Very Suitable	Less Suitable

Figure 11.9. Matrix for Answers to Question 4.

Generally speaking, you can also group the selection of which Automation Framework to use by the following rules-of-thumb:-

- Module Automation Framework is best suited to larger, more complex software, which have calculations, but less inputs. Systems which are mature and not likely to change.
- Data Driven Automation Frameworks are best suited for smaller software, which are less complex, but have larger amounts of inputs requiring more scenarios to test. Systems which is mature and not likely to change.

- Keyword Driven Automation Frameworks are best suited for larger software which can be complex. They are also suitable for larger number of inputs, reasonably suited for software that will change.
- Page Object Automation Frameworks are best suited to smaller software, which are less likely to change.

Chapter 12: Automated Testing discussion

Now is time to have a discussion of the benefits and drawbacks of automated testing

U p until this point in the book we have concentrated on

Selenium RC and how to perform automated testing using Selenium RC, but now is the correct time to have a discussion around automated testing in general, this will include:

- ✓ The benefits of Automated Testing.
- ✓ The drawbacks of Automated Testing.

12.1 Starting at the end?

Some of you will be asking: *why have this chapter so late on within this book?* The simple reason is that the objective of this book was to teach you to use Selenium RC, giving the pros-and-cons of automated testing early on would only succeed in clouding your view of automated testing, and may well have resulted in putting you off learning and using Selenium RC, resulting in the book failing, before you had even got to Chapter 3!

12.2 Advantages of Automated Testing

Automated testing has many, many benefits for both the Tester, the Testing Department, the Company performing the testing, and also the end Customer. Some of the benefits include:

- **Repeatability**: Tests can be repeated again and again.
- **Reliability**: Every time the test is ran the results produced will be consistent, unlike human testing which has the "human error" factor, automated testing will reliably test the same way each and every time.

- **Reduced Cost**: As the software grows over time, requiring more time/resources to test it thoroughly, automated testing will reduce the cost of hiring extra staff to complete the testing.
- **Reusability**: If done in the correct manor, the test scripts can be re-used with ease.
- **Skill Development**: Testers will learn new skills, and also enhance their existing skill set.

12.3 Dis-Advantages of Automated Testing

Automated testing has some drawbacks for both the Tester, the Testing Department, and the Company performing the testing. These include:

- **Cost**: In terms of both the costs of the time to implement the automated testing, the cost of training the staff to use the automated testing, and any costs related to new hardware/software requirements.
- **Maintenance**: Just like manual Test Scripts, automated Test Scripts will need to be maintained, and this will generally be more often and more time consuming than manual Test Scripts.
- **Complexity**: As well as the need to learn new skills to be able to create automated Test Scripts, the work needed to get them to run (particularly when they hit problems) can be extremely complex.
- **Re-work**: Simple changes to the User Interface of the software being tested can require the re-creation of whole Test Scripts.

12.4 Should you use Automated Testing?

So the question is **Is Automated Testing worth it?** And the answer is dependent on your circumstances. If the software you are testing is suitable for automated testing, you have the skills, and are eager to perform automated testing, then the answer is Automated Testing is 100% worth it!

12.5 Expectations for Automated Testing

Now let's set some realistic expectations for Automated Testing:-

- **Coverage**: Expect to get a maximum of 50-70% coverage of User Interface functionality. 100% is <u>not</u> realistic or achievable.
- **Increased time**: Expected, initially, that the Test Scripts will take considerably longer to create compared to manual Test Scripts. Budget for somewhere between 4 and 8 times as longer for the first six months, then reduce this to between 2 and 4 going forward.
- **Keep Manual Testing**: Although it may seem sensible to just drop manual testing, you will find you will still need to manually test.

Chapter 13: Automated Testing approach

Now is time to discuss how to approach the implementation of automated testing

N ow we can put some ideas together on how to approach

the implementation of Automated Testing. These include:

- ✓ Choosing what to automate.
- ✓ Validating the automated test results.
- ✓ Guidelines for the automated testing.

13.1 Choosing what to automate

It is often daunting to know what to automate, and where to start with automated testing. Some points to consider for the areas to automate:-

- **Repeated Tasks**: Tasks which are done again-and-again, offer the most saving.
- **Stable functionality**: Automated testing is best suited to mature and stable functionality, which is less-likely to change and break.
- **Well-defined functionality**: If you cannot describe what functionality should do (the expected outcome) you cannot automate the testing of this functionality. Only attempt to automate functionality that is well-defined, well-understood, and well-documented.

13.2 Validating the results

Once you have automated an area of functionality, you then need to confirm that the results produced by the automated testing are correct. For example, suppose we have automated the testing of a piece of functionality but the automated testing identifies none of the bugs that exist in this functionality, what value does is offer? None! You need to validate the automated test results against manual test results, and always build in the "missed" bugs, i.e. if automated testing missed a bug, add it as a scenario, so automated test never misses that bug again (or similar bugs)!

13.3 Guidelines for Automated Testing

To be successful, automated testing needs:-

- **Grown**: To be grown over time, don't try to automate everything from Day 1.
- **Foundation**: Create a foundation of simple Test functionality, and then build upon these simple Test functionality to be able to test more complex functionality.
- **Defined**: Clearly define every scenario you intend to test.
- **Value**: Offer value, there is no point spending 100 days automating something which would take 1 day to test!

Appendix A: **Selenium RC Commands**

This appendices list out the main functions available within Selenium RC. These are the basic functionality that is available to control Selenium RC and aid the automated testing you can perform.

To ease readability, the list of functions in Selenium RC are ordered alphabetically. To this, Chapter 7 lists out Selenium RC functions that you will find most useful.

Selenium RC Functions.
addLocationStrategy
addLocationStrategyAndWait
addScript
addScriptAndWait
addSelection
addSelectionAndWait
allowNativeXpath
allowNativeXpathAndWait
altKeyDown
altKeyDownAndWait
altKeyUp
altKeyUpAndWait
answerOnNextPrompt
assertAlert
assertAlertNotPresent
assertAlertPresent
assertAllButtons
assertAllFields
assertAllLinks
assertAllWindowIds
assertAllWindowNames
assertAllWindowTitles

assertAttribute
assertAttributeFromAllWindows
assertBodyText
assertChecked
assertConfirmation
assertConfirmationNotPresent
assertConfirmationPresent
assertCookie
assertCookieByName
assertCookieNotPresent
assertCookiePresent
assertCursorPosition
assertEditable
assertElementHeight
assertElementIndex
assertElementNotPresent
assertElementPositionLeft
assertElementPositionTop
assertElementPresent
assertElementWidth
assertEval
assertExpression
assertHtmlSource
assertLocation
assertMouseSpeed
assertNotAlert
assertNotAllButtons
assertNotAllFields
assertNotAllLinks
assertNotAllWindowIds
assertNotAllWindowNames

assertNotAllWindowTitles
assertNotAttribute
assertNotAttributeFromAllWindows
assertNotBodyText
assertNotChecked
assertNotConfirmation
assertNotCookie
assertNotCookieByName
assertNotCursorPosition
assertNotEditable
assertNotElementHeight
assertNotElementIndex
assertNotElementPositionLeft
assertNotElementPositionTop
assertNotElementWidth
assertNotEval
assertNotExpression
assertNotHtmlSource
assertNotLocation
assertNotMouseSpeed
assertNotOrdered
assertNotPrompt
assertNotSelectOptions
assertNotSelectedId
assertNotSelectedIds
assertNotSelectedIndex
assertNotSelectedIndexes
assertNotSelectedLabel
assertNotSelectedLabels
assertNotSelectedValue
assertNotSelectedValues

assertNotSomethingSelected
assertNotSpeed
assertNotTable
assertNotText
assertNotTitle
assertNotValue
assertNotVisible
assertNotWhetherThisFrameMatchFrameExpression
assertNotWhetherThisWindowMatchWindowExpression
assertNotXpathCount
assertOrdered
assertPrompt
assertPromptNotPresent
assertPromptPresent
assertSelectOptions
assertSelectedId
assertSelectedIds
assertSelectedIndex
assertSelectedIndexes
assertSelectedLabel
assertSelectedLabels
assertSelectedValue
assertSelectedValues
assertSomethingSelected
assertSpeed
assertTable
assertText
assertTextNotPresent
assertTextPresent
assertTitle

assertValue
assertVisible
assertWhetherThisFrameMatchFrameExpression
assertWhetherThisWindowMatchWindowExpression
assertXpathCount
assignId
assignIdAndWait
break
captureEntirePageScreenshot
captureEntirePageScreenshotAndWait
check
checkAndWait
chooseCancelOnNextConfirmation
chooseOkOnNextConfirmation
chooseOkOnNextConfirmationAndWait
click
clickAndWait
clickAt
clickAtAndWait
close
contextMenu
contextMenuAndWait
contextMenuAt
contextMenuAtAndWait
controlKeyDown
controlKeyDownAndWait
controlKeyUp
controlKeyUpAndWait
createCookie
createCookieAndWait
deleteAllVisibleCookies

deleteAllVisibleCookiesAndWait
deleteCookie
deleteCookieAndWait
deselectPopUp
deselectPopUpAndWait
doubleClick
doubleClickAndWait
doubleClickAt
doubleClickAtAndWait
dragAndDrop
dragAndDropAndWait
dragAndDropToObject
dragAndDropToObjectAndWait
dragdrop
dragdropAndWait
echo
fireEvent
fireEventAndWait
focus
focusAndWait
goBack
goBackAndWait
highlight
highlightAndWait
ignoreAttributesWithoutValue
ignoreAttributesWithoutValueAndWait
keyDown
keyDownAndWait
keyPress
keyPressAndWait
keyUp

keyUpAndWait
metaKeyDown
metaKeyDownAndWait
metaKeyUp
metaKeyUpAndWait
mouseDown
mouseDownAndWait
mouseDownAt
mouseDownAtAndWait
mouseDownRight
mouseDownRightAndWait
mouseDownRightAt
mouseDownRightAtAndWait
mouseMove
mouseMoveAndWait
mouseMoveAt
mouseMoveAtAndWait
mouseOut
mouseOutAndWait
mouseOver
mouseOverAndWait
mouseUp
mouseUpAndWait
mouseUpAt
mouseUpAtAndWait
mouseUpRight
mouseUpRightAndWait
mouseUpRightAt
mouseUpRightAtAndWait
open
openWindow

openWindowAndWait
pause
refresh
refreshAndWait
removeAllSelections
removeAllSelectionsAndWait
removeScript
removeScriptAndWait
removeSelection
removeSelectionAndWait
rollup
rollupAndWait
runScript
runScriptAndWait
select
selectAndWait
selectFrame
selectPopUp
selectPopUpAndWait
selectWindow
sendKeys
setBrowserLogLevel
setBrowserLogLevelAndWait
setCursorPosition
setCursorPositionAndWait
setMouseSpeed
setMouseSpeedAndWait
setSpeed
setSpeedAndWait
setTimeout
shiftKeyDown

shiftKeyDownAndWait
shiftKeyUp
shiftKeyUpAndWait
store
storeAlert
storeAlertPresent
storeAllButtons
storeAllFields
storeAllLinks
storeAllWindowIds
storeAllWindowNames
storeAllWindowTitles
storeAttribute
storeAttributeFromAllWindows
storeBodyText
storeChecked
storeConfirmation
storeConfirmationPresent
storeCookie
storeCookieByName
storeCookiePresent
storeCursorPosition
storeEditable
storeElementHeight
storeElementIndex
storeElementPositionLeft
storeElementPositionTop
storeElementPresent
storeElementWidth
storeEval
storeExpression

storeHtmlSource
storeLocation
storeMouseSpeed
storeOrdered
storePrompt
storePromptPresent
storeSelectOptions
storeSelectedId
storeSelectedIds
storeSelectedIndex
storeSelectedIndexes
storeSelectedLabel
storeSelectedLabels
storeSelectedValue
storeSelectedValues
storeSomethingSelected
storeSpeed
storeTable
storeText
storeTextPresent
storeTitle
storeValue
storeVisible
storeWhetherThisFrameMatchFrameExpression
storeWhetherThisWindowMatchWindowExpression
storeXpathCount
submit
submitAndWait
type
typeAndWait
typeKeys

typeKeysAndWait
uncheck
uncheckAndWait
useXpathLibrary
useXpathLibraryAndWait
verifyAlert
verifyAlertNotPresent
verifyAlertPresent
verifyAllButtons
verifyAllFields
verifyAllLinks
verifyAllWindowIds
verifyAllWindowNames
verifyAllWindowTitles
verifyAttribute
verifyAttributeFromAllWindows
verifyBodyText
verifyChecked
verifyConfirmation
verifyConfirmationNotPresent
verifyConfirmationPresent
verifyCookie
verifyCookieByName
verifyCookieNotPresent
verifyCookiePresent
verifyCursorPosition
verifyEditable
verifyElementHeight
verifyElementIndex
verifyElementNotPresent
verifyElementPositionLeft

verifyElementPositionTop
verifyElementPresent
verifyElementWidth
verifyEval
verifyExpression
verifyHtmlSource
verifyLocation
verifyMouseSpeed
verifyNotAlert
verifyNotAllButtons
verifyNotAllFields
verifyNotAllLinks
verifyNotAllWindowIds
verifyNotAllWindowNames
verifyNotAllWindowTitles
verifyNotAttribute
verifyNotAttributeFromAllWindows
verifyNotBodyText
verifyNotChecked
verifyNotConfirmation
verifyNotCookie
verifyNotCookieByName
verifyNotCursorPosition
verifyNotEditable
verifyNotElementHeight
verifyNotElementIndex
verifyNotElementPositionLeft
verifyNotElementPositionTop
verifyNotElementWidth
verifyNotEval
verifyNotExpression

verifyNotHtmlSource
verifyNotLocation
verifyNotMouseSpeed
verifyNotOrdered
verifyNotPrompt
verifyNotSelectOptions
verifyNotSelectedId
verifyNotSelectedIds
verifyNotSelectedIndex
verifyNotSelectedIndexes
verifyNotSelectedLabel
verifyNotSelectedLabels
verifyNotSelectedValue
verifyNotSelectedValues
verifyNotSomethingSelected
verifyNotSpeed
verifyNotTable
verifyNotText
verifyNotTitle
verifyNotValue
verifyNotVisible
verifyNotWhetherThisFrameMatchFrameExpression
verifyNotWhetherThisWindowMatchWindowExpression
verifyNotXpathCount
verifyOrdered
verifyPrompt
verifyPromptNotPresent
verifyPromptPresent
verifySelectOptions
verifySelectedId

verifySelectedIds
verifySelectedIndex
verifySelectedLabel
verifySelectedLabels
verifySelectedValue
verifySelectedValues
verifySomethingSelected
verifySpeed
verifyTable
verifyText
verifyTextNotPresent
verifyTextPresent
verifyTitle
verifyValue
verifyVisible
verifyWhetherThisFrameMatchFrameExpression
verifyWhetherThisWindowMatchWindowExpression
verifyXpathCount
waitForAlert
waitForAlertNotPresent
waitForAlertPresent
waitForAllButtons
waitForAllFields
waitForAllLinks
waitForAllWindowIds
waitForAllWindowNames
waitForAllWindowTitles
waitForAttribute
waitForAttributeFromAllWindows
waitForBodyText
waitForChecked

waitForCondition
waitForConfirmation
waitForConfirmationNotPresent
waitForConfirmationPresent
waitForCookie
waitForCookieByName
waitForCookieNotPresent
waitForCookiePresent
waitForCursorPosition
waitForEditable
waitForElementHeight
waitForElementIndex
waitForElementNotPresent
waitForElementPositionLeft
waitForElementPositionTop
waitForElementPresent
waitForElementWidth
waitForEval
waitForExpression
waitForFrameToLoad
waitForHtmlSource
waitForLocation
waitForMouseSpeed
waitForNotAlert
waitForNotAllButtons
waitForNotAllFields
waitForNotAllLinks
waitForNotAllWindowIds
waitForNotAllWindowNames
waitForNotAllWindowTitles
waitForNotAttribute

waitForNotAttributeFromAllWindows
waitForNotBodyText
waitForNotChecked
waitForNotConfirmation
waitForNotCookie
waitForNotCookieByName
waitForNotCursorPosition
waitForNotEditable
waitForNotElementHeight
waitForNotElementIndex
waitForNotElementPositionLeft
waitForNotElementPositionTop
waitForNotElementWidth
waitForNotEval
waitForNotExpression
waitForNotHtmlSource
waitForNotLocation
waitForNotMouseSpeed
waitForNotOrdered
waitForNotPrompt
waitForNotSelectOptions
waitForNotSelectedId
waitForNotSelectedIds
waitForNotSelectedIndex
waitForNotSelectedIndexes
waitForNotSelectedLabel
waitForNotSelectedLabels
waitForNotSelectedValue
waitForNotSelectedValues
waitForNotSomethingSelected
waitForNotSpeed

waitForNotTable
waitForNotText
waitForNotTitle
waitForNotValue
waitForNotVisible
waitForNotWhetherThisFrameMatchFrameExpression
waitForNotWhetherThisWindowMatchWindowExpression
waitForNotXpathCount
waitForOrdered
waitForPageToLoad
waitForPopUp
waitForPrompt
waitForPromptNotPresent
waitForPromptPresent
waitForSelectOptions
waitForSelectedId
waitForSelectedIds
waitForSelectedIndex
waitForSelectedIndexes
waitForSelectedLabel
waitForSelectedLabels
waitForSelectedValue
waitForSelectedValues
waitForSomethingSelected
waitForSpeed
waitForTable
waitForText
waitForTextNotPresent
waitForTextPresent

waitForTitle
waitForValue
waitForVisible
waitForWhetherThisFrameMatchFrameExpression
waitForWhetherThisWindowMatchWindowExpression
waitForXpathCount
windowFocus
windowFocusAndWait
windowMaximize
windowMaximizeAndWait

Appendix B: List of Figures

Below is a list of the Figures used in this book, and their corresponding Page number. To aid readability, these have been split by Chapters.

Chapter 7:

Below are the list of Figures shown in Chapter 7 of this book:

Figure 7.1 The Click function

Figure 7.2 The ClickAt function

Figure 7.3 The Focus function

Figure 7.4 The Highlight function

Figure 7.5 The KeyDown function

Figure 7.6 The MouseDownAt function

Figure 7.7 The Type function

Figure 7.8 Syntax of declaring a Variable without setting the data

Figure 7.9 Declaring a variable

Figure 7.10 Syntax of declaring a Variable with setting the data

Figure 7.11 Declaring a variable

Chapter 9:

Below are the list of Figures shown in Chapter 9 of this book:

Figure 9.1 Using the Identifier method on the name attribute.

Figure 9.2 Using the Identifier method on the id attribute.

Figure 9.3 Using the Id method.

Figure 9.4 Using the Name method.

Figure 9.5 Using the Link method.

Figure 9.6 Using the DOM method.

Figure 9.7 Using the CSS method.

Figure 9.8 Using the Xpath method.

Chapter 10:

Below are the list of Figures shown in Chapter 10 of this book:

Figure 10.1 Automated Test Script recommended approach

Figure 10.2 Automated Test Script recommended structure

Chapter 11:

Below are the list of Figures shown in Chapter 11 of this book:

About The Author

Mark Chatham is an IT professional, who has been working in the IT industry for 15 years. His education background includes both BSc and MSc Degrees in
Computer Science, as well MCP and ISEB professional Certifications.

During his professional IT career he has gained experience in the following technologies:

Development Langauges:
C, C++, C#, Java, Visual Basic.NET, SQL, XML.

Database Management Systems:
Microsoft SQL Server, Sybase SQL Anywhere, Microsoft Access, Ingres SQL.

Automation Testing Tools:
Selenium IDE, RC, Web Driver, QTP, Telerik Web UI, InCisif .NET, JMeter, OWASP.

The author can be contacted via email on:
mchatham@hotmail.co.uk

(Please ensure any comments or questions relating to this book, have the Subject text of "**Selenium By Example – Volume I: Selenium RC**").

Related Titles

The following titles are from the **Selenium By Example** series of books, and are from the same author:

- **Selenium By Example – Volume I: Selenium IDE.**
  This title gives a step-by-step overview of Selenium IDE.

- **Selenium By Example – Volume III: Selenium WebDriver.**
  This title gives a step-by-step overview of Selenium WebDriver.

All title follow the same example based method to teach the reader the necessary information in a step-by-step way. This is to ensure that the reader is able to quickly and efficiently learn the new information presented. The following titles